A BOOK FOR MY
Daughter

PAMELA WINTERBOURNE

WELLERAN POLTARNEES

LAUGHING ELEPHANT   MMIII

ISBN 1-883211-54-9

SECOND PRINTING ALL RIGHTS RESERVED
PRINTED IN SINGAPORE

LAUGHING ELEPHANT BOOKS
3645 INTERLAKE AVENUE NORTH   SEATTLE   98103

www.LAUGHINGELEPHANT.com

Dear Daughter,

I send you this book because it
expresses the love I feel for you.

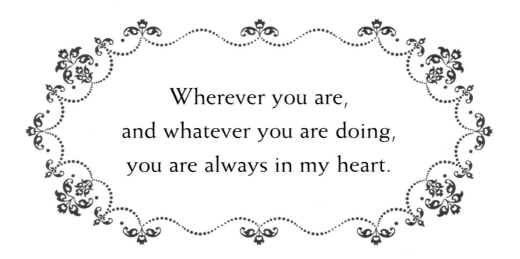

Wherever you are,
and whatever you are doing,
you are always in my heart.

3

Let us never forget the wonderful
times we have had together –

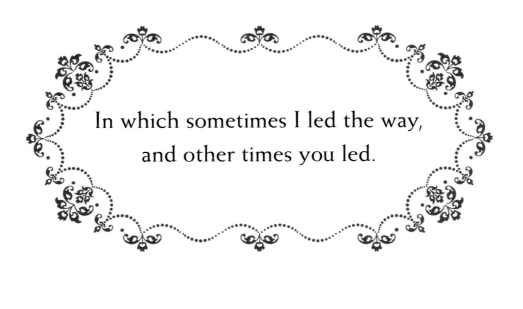

In which sometimes I led the way,
and other times you led.

May there always be places
for you to attain peace.

9

Savor the myriad
small pleasures of life.

May you have
many moments of success.

Let the things you own
be lovely, and your enjoyment
of them fulfilling.

15

I know you will keep alive
your capacity for wonder
and delight.

17

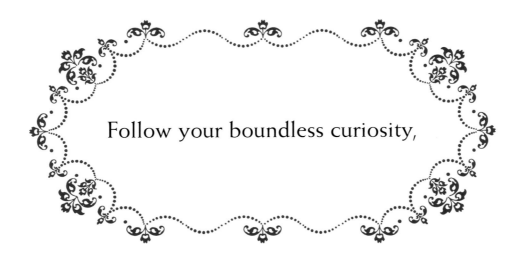

Follow your boundless curiosity,

19

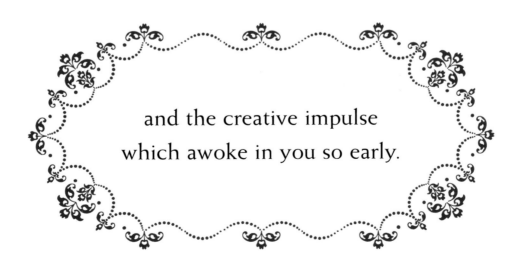

and the creative impulse
which awoke in you so early.

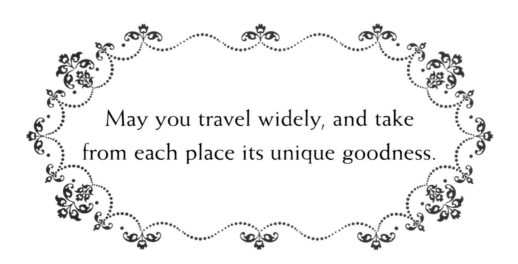

May you travel widely, and take
from each place its unique goodness.

23

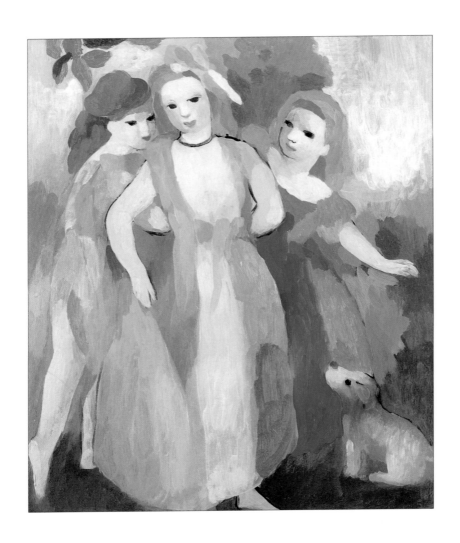

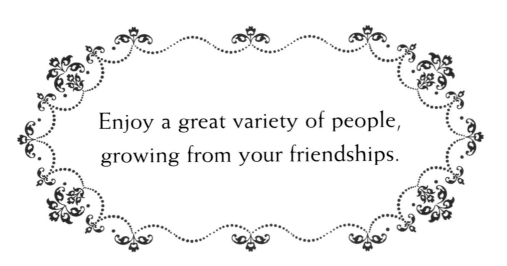

Enjoy a great variety of people,
growing from your friendships.

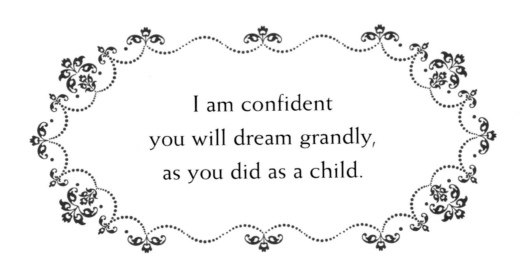

I am confident
you will dream grandly,
as you did as a child.

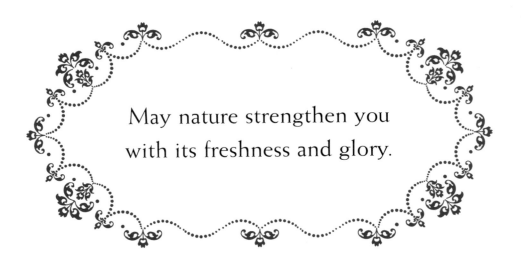

May nature strengthen you
with its freshness and glory.

29

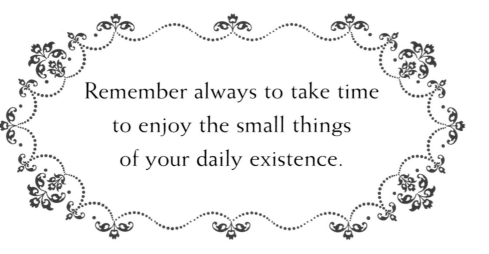

Remember always to take time
to enjoy the small things
of your daily existence.

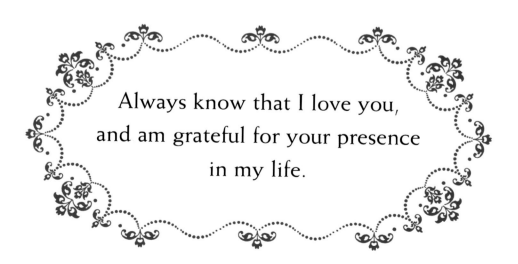

Always know that I love you,
and am grateful for your presence
in my life.

Daffodil Garden

List of Species and Varieties shown on endpapers

1. Double Yellow.
2. Rugulosus (odorus).
3. Mrs. J. B. M. Camm.
4 . Tazetta ochroleuca.
5 and 5A. Queen of Spain.
6. Cynosure.
7. Muticus.
8. Tazetta orielitalis.
9. Backhousei.
10. Poeticus ornatus.
11. Queen Sophia.
12. Stella.
13. New seedling.
14. Poeticus radiiflorus.
15. Macleayi tridymus.
16. Marie M. de Graaf.
17. Santa Maria.
18. Astraea.
19. Burbidgei, Falstaff.
20. Cernuus.
21. Jonquilla.
22. Madge Matthews.
23. Rev. T. J. Berkeley.
24. Paper white.

25. Bicolor Horsfieldii.
26. Ellen Willmott.
27. Gloriosa.
28. Sulphureus plenus.
29. Poeticus.
30. Emperor.
31. Bicolor grandis.
32. Burbidgei, Ariel.
33. Colleen Bawn.
34. Sir Watkin.
35. Incomparabilis splendens.
36. Hoop Petticoat (Corbularia monophylla).
37. Calathinus.
38. Cyclamineus.
39. Triandrus albus.
40. Mi or.
41. Bulbocodium citrinum.
42. Triandrus.
43. Albus.
44. Nelsoni major.
45. Empress.
46. Princess Mary.
47. W. P. Milner.
48. Hume's Giant.

49. Frank Miles.
50. Minnie Hume.
51. Michael Foster.
52. Tazetta chinensis.
53. Poculiformis.
54. Gracilis tenuior.
55. John Ball.
56. Cernuus concolor.
57. Bulbocodium.
58 Juncifolius.
59. Queen of the Netherlands.
60. Leedsii, Aladdin.
61. Triandrus tricolor.
62. C. J. Backhouse.
63. Fanny Mason.
64. Little Dirk.
65. Barri, Sensation.
66. Butter and Eggs (Golden Phoenix).
67. Leedsii, Lanthe.
68. Albert Victor.
69. Amabilis.
70. Beatrice.
71. Titan.

Picture Credits

Cover	Helen Turner. "Girl With Lantern," 1904.
Endpapers	John Allen. From *The Boys Own Annual*, 1901.
Half-title	Childe Hassam. "Lilies," 1910.
Frontispiece	Charles Courtney Curran. "The West Wind," 1918.
Title Page	L. Hummel. From *Letty: A Study of a Child*, 1927.
2	William Vincent Cahill. "Thoughts of the Sea," 1919.
3	Edmund G. Schildknecht. "Seated Figure," 1929.
4	Jessie Willcox Smith.
5	Maurice Denis. "La Couronne de Marguerites," c. 1905.
6	Charles Courtney Curran. "Wind Driven Clouds," 1928.
7	Leon Droll. "Sandra and Marie Claude," c. 1937.
8	Thea Proctor. "The Sun Room," c. 1940.
9	Guy Rose. "La Jolla Arbor," n.d.
10	Anonymous magazine cover, 1932.
11	Henri Le Sidaner. "La Table Sur La Cour," 1926.
12	John H. McCracken. Magazine cover, 1915.
13	W.T. Benda. Magazine cover, 1934.
14	Frederick C. Frieseke. "The Gold Locket," c. 1917.
15	Guy Rose. "From the Dining Room Window," c. 1910.
16	Rockwell Kent. "Annie McGinley," 1926.
17	Carl Larsson. "Lille-Anna og Krokusserne," 1912.
18	Childe Hassam. "Couch on the Porch, Cos Cob," 1914.
19	Harold Knight. "The Morning Sun," n.d.
20	H.R. Robertson. From *More Plants We Play With*, 1920.
21	Anonymous magazine advertisement, 1923.
22	Anonymous travel advertisement, n.d.
23	Jupp Wiertz. Poster, c. 1937.
24	Marie Laurencin. "Trois Filles," n.d.
25	Frank Gensing. Magazine cover, 1931.
26	Robert Henri. "Little Dreamer," n.d.
27	McMein. Magazine cover, 1930.
28	Camille Bombois. "Nympheas sur L'Etang de la Ville D'Avray," n.d.
29	Haskell Coffin. Magazine cover, 1927.
30	Louis Ritman. "Freshly Picked Flowers," 1914.
31	C. Coles Phillips. Magazine cover, 1920.
32	Walter Howell Deverell. "Heads of Two Women, One Kissing the Other," 1853.
33	Maurice Denis. "Ce fût un religieux mystère," 1898.
34	John Allen. From *The Boys Own Annual*, 1901
Back Cover	Adrian Feint. "House and Flame Tree," 1941.